WELSH HISTORY

BETSI CADW
A VICTORIAN NURSE

JOHN EVANS

Illustrated by Rob Chapman

Powys

DREF WEN

Betsi Cadwaladr was born
on a farm near Bala
in the year 1789.

Her mother died
when she was 5 years old
and her big sister
had to take care of her.

3

When she was 9 years old,
Betsi went to work for a rich man
named Simon Lloyd.

She cleaned the house
and made the beds.
She worked very hard.

Mr Lloyd was a kind man.
He taught Betsi how to
read, write, and play the harp.

But Betsi was bored with Bala.
"I want to see the world,"
she said.

When she was 14 years old,
Betsi ran away to Liverpool.

She soon began to see the world, because she worked as a servant to a rich family.

She visited London, France
and then Italy.

Then she became a servant
to a sea captain
and sailed all around the world.

She visited India, Africa,
Australia and China,
and saw many wonderful things.

Betsi travelled for many years.
At last she said,
"I am getting too old to travel.
It is time to settle down."

One day, Betsi read in the newspaper
about a war in the Crimea.
Many soldiers were wounded
and needed help.

Betsi said, "I will become a nurse and help the soldiers."

Betsi put on her grey dress,
grey cloak and brown bonnet,
and sailed to the war.
She worked in a hospital
run by Florence Nightingale.

16

But Betsi was not happy.
She said, "We are still too far away
from where the soldiers are fighting."
Florence said, "You cannot go closer.
It is too dangerous for women."

17

Betsi said, "Nonsense!"
and ran off to Balaclava,
the place in the Crimea
where the soldiers were fighting.

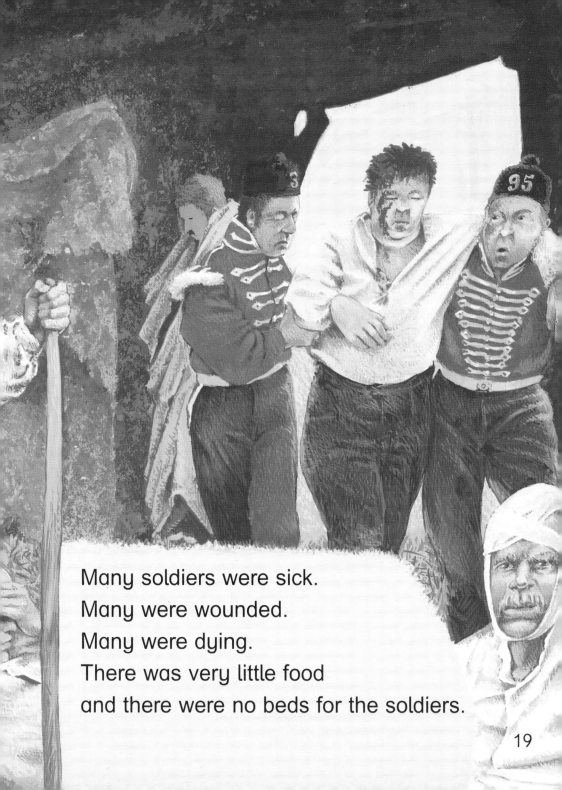

Many soldiers were sick.
Many were wounded.
Many were dying.
There was very little food
and there were no beds for the soldiers.

Betsi found food and beds.
She helped many of the soldiers
to get better.

Then Betsi herself caught a fever
and had to be sent home.
The soldiers were sad
to see her leave.

Betsi had become weak and poor.
She had spent all her money
helping the soldiers.

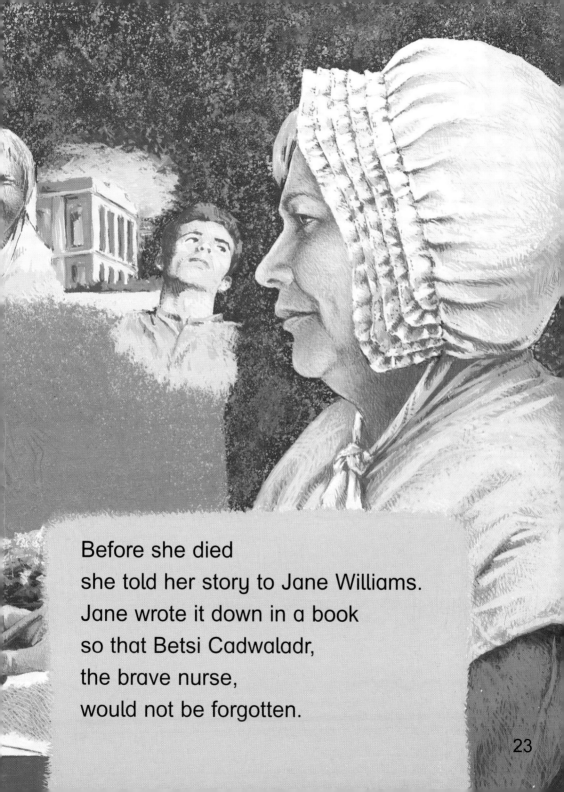

Before she died
she told her story to Jane Williams.
Jane wrote it down in a book
so that Betsi Cadwaladr,
the brave nurse,
would not be forgotten.

INDEX